CW00797193

The
SMALL and MIGHTY
Book of
The
Human Body

Tom Jackson and Kirsti Davidson

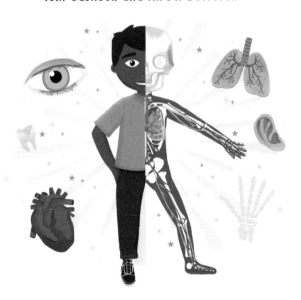

Published in 2022 by OH!,
An imprint of Welbeck Children's Limited, part of Welbeck Publishing Group
Based in London and Sydney.

www.welbeckpublishing.com

A CIP catalogue record for this book is available from the British Library.

Writer: Tom Jackson
Illustrator: Kirsti Davidson
Design and text by Raspberry Books Ltd
Project Manager: Russell Porter
Editorial Manager: Joff Brown
Design Manager: Matt Drew
Production: Jess Brisley

ISBN 978 1 83935 177 8

Printed in Heshan, China

10 9 8 7 6 5 4 3 2 1

The
SMALL and MIGHTY
Book of
The
Human Body

Tom Jackson and Kirsti Davidson

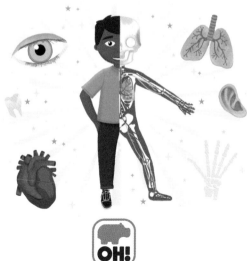

Contents

Transport
Systems
79

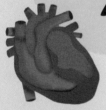

Attack and
Defence
125

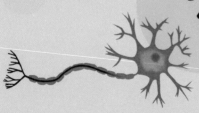

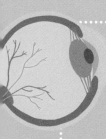

INTRODUCTION

∽

This little book is absolutely bursting with facts about the human body.

Our bodies are amazing machines made from billions of parts. They are all working perfectly together, keeping you on the move and having fun!

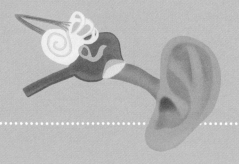

In this book you will discover . . .

🗩 How much poo you produce in a lifetime (and why it's brown)

🗩 The mind-boggling number of connections there are in your brain

🗩 How your fingers move even though they contain no muscles

🗩 The proper name for earwax.

. . . and lots more.

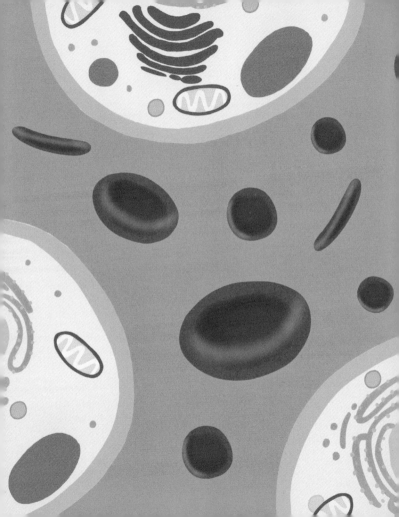

Body Building Blocks

~ THE ~
HUMAN BODY

is built from tiny building
blocks called cells.
There are about 37 trillion –

37,000,000,000,000

– of them in an adult's body.

cell

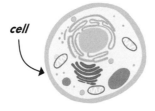

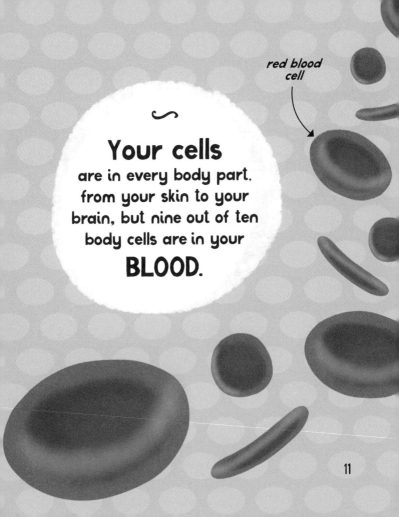

red blood
cell

Your cells
are in every body part,
from your skin to your
brain, but nine out of ten
body cells are in your
BLOOD.

11

EVERY CELL IN THE BODY HAS
A PARTICULAR JOB. SOME CELLS
MAKE BONE OR MUSCLES, WHILE
OTHERS DEAL WITH YOUR FOOD OR
DEFEND THE BODY FROM ATTACK.

NEARLY ALL OF THEM ARE TOO
SMALL TO SEE WITHOUT A
POWERFUL MICROSCOPE.

The very
smallest cells are found
in the **BACK OF THE BRAIN.**
They are so tiny that 250 would
line up on the full stop at the
end of this sentence.

~

The LARGEST cells are the long nerve cells
in the legs. These can be 1 metre long!

13

About
two-thirds
of your body is
made up of water.
Most of the water is
held inside each cell
and has many other
chemicals mixed
into it.

Almost all of your body is made up of just six simple substances called elements.

If you weigh 40 kg then your body contains . . .

26 kg of oxygen

7.2 kg of carbon

4 kg of hydrogen

1.2 kg of nitrogen

600 g of calcium

440 g of phosphorus

The rest of you is made up of tiny amounts of 16 other elements, including **IRON, SODIUM** and **CHLORINE.**

BODY CELLS

are like tiny bags. Inside there are miniature objects that do different jobs in the cell, help keep it alive and working properly.

cell

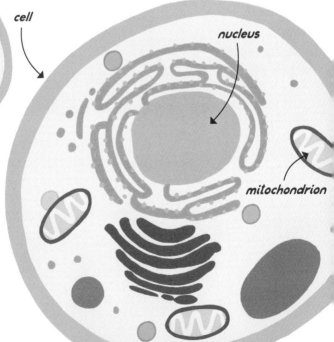

nucleus

mitochondrion

One of these objects is the
MITOCHONDRION.
This gives the cell its energy.

The mitochondrion works
like the cell's power station,
burning sugar to
release energy.

17

nucleus

THE NUCLEUS IS THE CONTROL CENTRE OF THE CELL.

~

It holds a chemical called DNA. DNA contains the genes, the instructions for how to build every part of a human body.

∽ A ∽

HUMAN BODY CELL

holds 2 m of DNA. If all the DNA in your body was joined together it would be 6 billion km long!

THAT'S ENOUGH TO GO TO THE SUN AND BACK 20 TIMES OVER!

DNA

THE CELLS IN THE BODY

work together in body parts called organs. Each organ carries out a particular set of jobs that keeps the body strong and healthy.

THE MAIN ORGANS ARE:

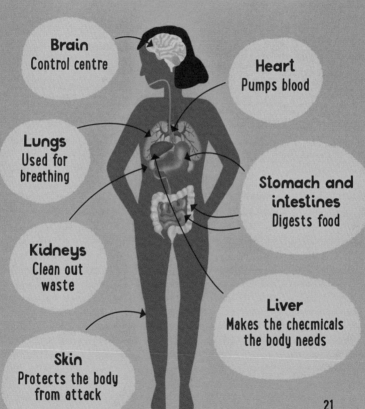

Brain
Control centre

Heart
Pumps blood

Lungs
Used for breathing

Stomach and intestines
Digests food

Kidneys
Clean out waste

Liver
Makes the checmicals the body needs

Skin
Protects the body from attack

21

Growing

THE **HUMAN BODY** IS
MAKING NEW CELLS
AND GROWING AND
CHANGING ALL THE
TIME. YOUR BODY
MAKES AN AMAZING
3.8 MILLION NEW
CELLS EVERY SECOND!

THE **BRAIN** IS ONE OF THE
FIRST BODY PARTS TO GROW. IT
IS ALREADY A THIRD OF FULL SIZE
WHEN A BABY IS BORN.

~

THE BRAIN REACHES ITS FULL SIZE
OF 1.3 KG WHEN A PERSON IS
20 YEARS OLD, BUT ITS MANY BRAIN
CELLS ARE STILL BEING WIRED
TOGETHER FOR ALL OF THEIR LIFE.

egg cell

~

YOU START GROWING

even before you are born. Human life
starts with special cells: the egg cell
and sperm cell. Women make egg cells in
their bodies and men make sperm cells.
One egg and one sperm join together
into a single cell, which then grows
and grows in the woman's body to
become a baby.

~

sperm cell

THE EGG CELL
IS A VERY LARGE CELL.
YOU CAN JUST ABOUT
SEE IT WITHOUT
A MICROSCOPE.

~

THE SPERM
IS ONE OF THE SMALLEST
CELLS IN THE BODY.
IT USES ITS TAIL TO SWIM
AND CAN TRAVEL AT
2.5 CM AN HOUR!

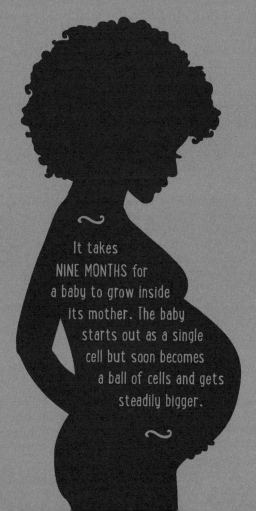

It takes
NINE MONTHS for
a baby to grow inside
its mother. The baby
starts out as a single
cell but soon becomes
a ball of cells and gets
steadily bigger.

28

ONE MONTH:
Baby is the size
of an apple seed

TWO MONTHS:
Strawberry

THREE MONTHS:
Peach

EIGHT MONTHS:
Honeydew melon

NINE MONTHS:
Watermelon –
time to be born!

FOUR MONTHS:
Pear

SEVEN MONTHS:
Coconut

SIX MONTHS:
Grapefruit

FIVE MONTHS:
Mango

29

YOU GROW FASTEST
WHEN YOU'RE A BABY.

By its FIRST birthday a baby
is double the size it was when
it was born. At the age of TWO,
the child is already around half
its adult height. At age 10 it
is half its adult weight.

~

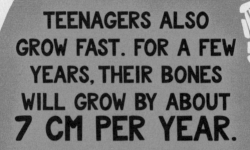

TEENAGERS ALSO GROW FAST. FOR A FEW YEARS, THEIR BONES WILL GROW BY ABOUT **7 CM PER YEAR.** THE LEGS START GETTING LONGER FIRST, AND THE UPPER BODY CATCHES UP LATER!

31

32

ZZZZZ

YOUR BODY DOES A LOT OF ITS GROWING AT NIGHT WHEN YOU ARE ASLEEP.

A newborn baby sleeps on and off for 20 hours a day.
A teenager needs about nine hours, while adults
generally need seven to eight hours of sleep a night.

You are about 1 cm shorter at night than in the morning
because your body weight has squashed your back
and knee joints a little. After a good night's sleep
you'll have stretched out again.

33

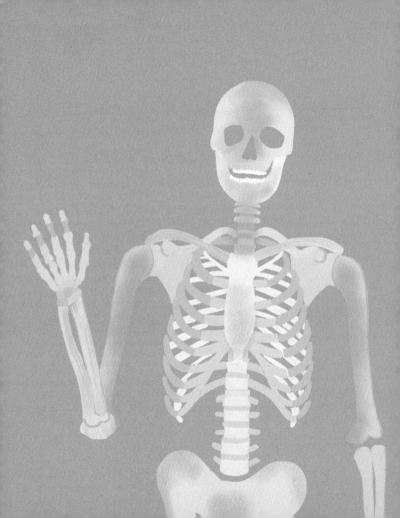

Bones and Muscles

~ THE ~
SKELETON
is the body's support system.

The hard bones give the body its shape. Without them, all the other body parts would flop into a squidgy blob.

~

There are 206 BONES in an adult's skeleton. When a baby is born it has 270 BONES, but these join together as the baby grows, making the bones thicker and the skeleton stronger.

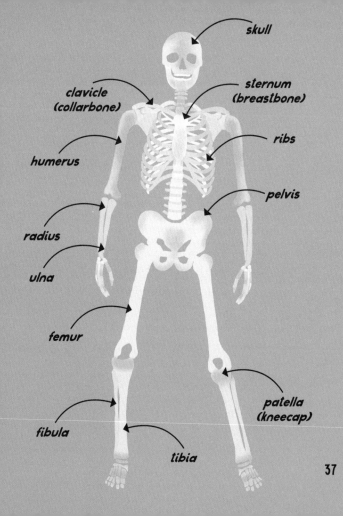

skull

clavicle
(collarbone)

sternum
(breastbone)

humerus

ribs

radius

pelvis

ulna

femur

patella
(kneecap)

fibula

tibia

37

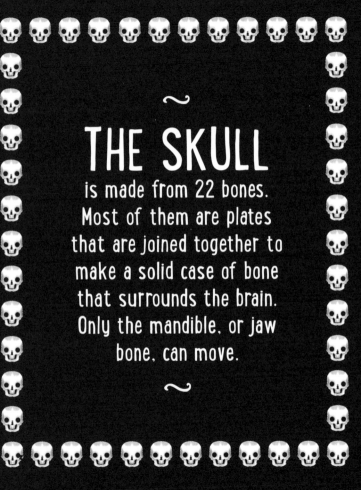

THE SKULL

is made from 22 bones.
Most of them are plates
that are joined together to
make a solid case of bone
that surrounds the brain.
Only the mandible, or jaw
bone, can move.

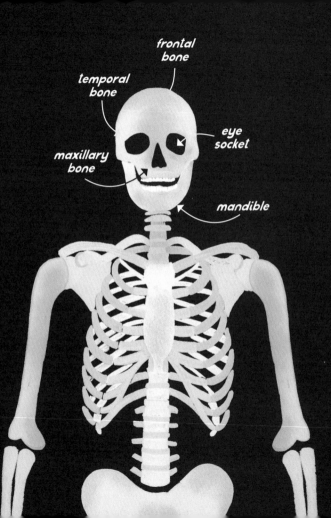

THE COLLARBONE IS
THE MOST COMMONLY
BROKEN BONE IN THE
BODY. ITS PROPER NAME
IS THE CLAVICLE, AND
THE TWO CLAVICLES
CONNECT THE RIBCAGE
TO THE SHOULDERS.

clavicle

clavicle

Bones are good at holding weight,
but can **BREAK**
if they are twisted or hit hard.

New bone grows to fill the gap created
by the break. After a few weeks the bone
is mended, but it can take about a year
for the bone to be strong again.

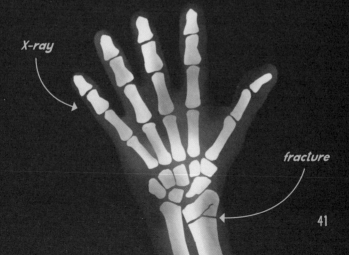

X-ray

fracture

The ribcage is made of 12 pairs of curved ribs that stick out from the spine and create a bony barrier around the softer organs, including the lungs, heart and stomach.

THE BACKBONE,

or spine, is made up of 33 smaller bones called vertebras. They are all stacked up to make a column that can twist and bend in all directions.

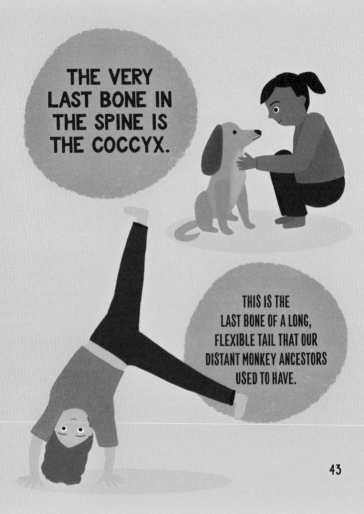

43

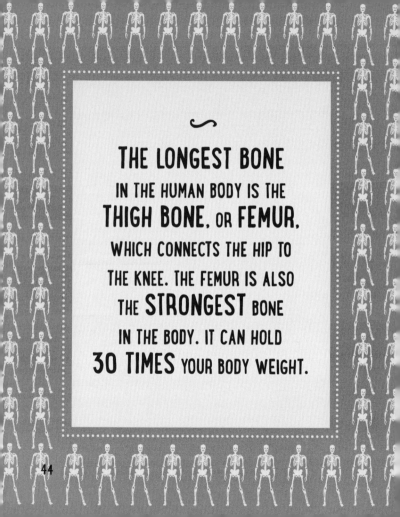

THE LONGEST BONE
IN THE HUMAN BODY IS THE
THIGH BONE, OR FEMUR,
WHICH CONNECTS THE HIP TO
THE KNEE. THE FEMUR IS ALSO
THE STRONGEST BONE
IN THE BODY. IT CAN HOLD
30 TIMES YOUR BODY WEIGHT.

THE BONES IN YOUR BODY
ARE VERY MUCH **ALIVE.**
MOST BONES ARE NOT SOLID
ALL THE WAY THROUGH.
INSTEAD THEY HAVE A
HONEYCOMB STRUCTURE.
THIS MAKES THEM **STRONG**
AND **FLEXIBLE** BUT ALSO
LIGHTWEIGHT.

MUSCLES MAKE YOUR BODY MOVE!

~

They are made of strong, stringy fibres that pull parts of your body around.

THERE ARE AROUND 650 MUSCLES IN THE HUMAN BODY.

SMALLEST: stapedius, inside the ear

LARGEST: gluteus maximus, in your bottom

STRONGEST: masseter (jaw muscle)

THERE ARE **43 MUSCLES** IN OUR FACE. WE USE THEM TO PULL ALL KINDS OF **EXPRESSIONS** ~ FROM ~ SMILING TO FROWNING.

47

THERE ARE THREE TYPES OF MUSCLE:

1. skeletal muscles – which are attached to bones and are used to move the body around

2. smooth muscle – found in the lining of the stomach and intestines and in blood cells

3. cardiac muscle – which keeps your heart beating (these muscles never rest).

It takes **200 MUSCLES** to take one step while walking. When we walk, one foot is always on the ground.

When we start **RUNNING**, both feet are off the ground most of the time. Each step is really a long leap forward.

49

muscle pulling
to bend arm

elbow
joint

muscle relaxed
while the other pulls

MUSCLES
are attached to the **BONES**.
Movement happens at a
JOINT where two bones meet,
such as the elbow. Muscles
always work in pairs, with one
bending the joint and the other
straightening it again.

Muscles work by getting shorter and
wider, which makes them **PULL** on the
bone. A muscle can only pull, never push.

The bones at the joint are held
in place by tough stretchy
bands called ligaments.

THE HANDS AND FEET
HAVE 106 BONES IN
THEM. EACH HAND
HAS 27 BONES, WHILE
EACH FOOT HAS 26.
THAT MEANS MORE
THAN HALF OF ALL
THE BODY'S BONES
ARE IN THE HANDS
AND FEET!

All those bones inside
the fingers and thumbs
make them really good at
moving around, touching and
holding things. However,
there are no muscles at
all inside the fingers or
thumb. They are moved by
muscles in the forearm and
palm of the hand instead.

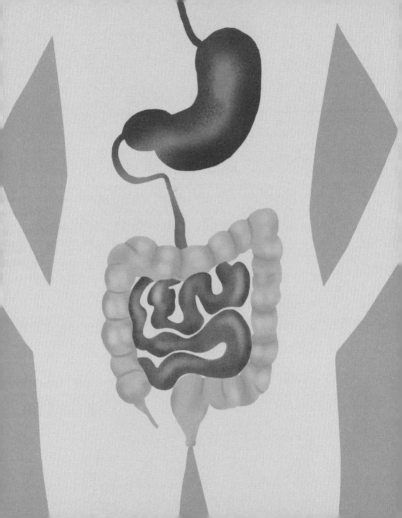

Eating
and
Digestion

~ THE ~ DIGESTIVE SYSTEM,

ALSO CALLED THE GUT, IS A LONG TUBE THAT RUNS FROM YOUR MOUTH TO YOUR BOTTOM. THE GUT'S JOB IS TO TAKE IN FOOD, ABSORB ALL ITS GOODNESS, AND GET RID OF THE UNWANTED WASTE AS POO.

~

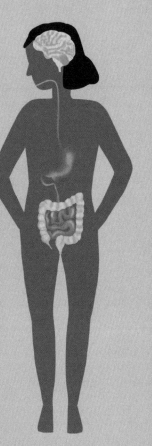

The digestive system starts at the mouth,

where the food is chewed by the teeth and mixed with saliva to make a smooth paste.

Every day an adult produces about 1 litre of saliva, but a toddler can make even more!

When you are six, your mouth has **52 teeth!** Only the 20 "milk teeth" can be seen. Your **32 adult** teeth are hidden in the jaw and skull. Soon the milk teeth will begin falling out, and the bigger adult teeth will move to take their place.

TOOTH ENAMEL, the white outer coating of the teeth, is the hardest stuff in the body — harder even than steel. (That's why you don't scratch your teeth while eating with a fork.)

But enamel is brittle, meaning it will crack into pieces quite easily.

59

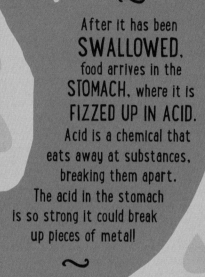

After it has been
SWALLOWED,
food arrives in the
STOMACH, where it is
FIZZED UP IN ACID.
Acid is a chemical that
eats away at substances,
breaking them apart.
The acid in the stomach
is so strong it could break
up pieces of metal!

The **STOMACH** is a big bag of muscle that can hold 1.3 litres (in an adult), which is about four cans of drink. Its job is to shake up the food and turn it into a soft, soupy goo. Food spends about four hours in the stomach.

After the stomach, food moves to the small **INTESTINE**. This is a long, narrow tube, about 7 m long but only 3 cm wide.

large intestine

It's coiled **UP** so it all fits inside you.

small intestine

The total length of an adult's gut is 9 m.

Food moving through
the small intestine is broken
down into smaller parts.

The useful parts get absorbed into
the blood vessels through the
intestine's lining, which is covered
in billions of tiny finger-like bumps.

If it could be smoothed flat, the small
intestine lining would cover about
a sixth of a tennis court!

The food absorbed by the intestines passes into the blood and goes to the **LIVER**, which organises all the different food chemicals before they are sent out into the rest of the body.

The liver is the heaviest organ inside the body. An adult's liver is 1.6kg, which is like carrying around four tins of beans!

The waste left behind from the food moves along to the 1.5-m large intestine.

The waste stays in here for 12 hours as the water is sucked out of it, leaving behind solid lumps of poo.

There are four main substances in foods:

~

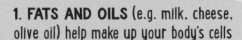

1. FATS AND OILS (e.g. milk, cheese, olive oil) help make up your body's cells

2. CARBOHYDRATES (e.g. bread, rice and other grains, potatoes, sugary foods, honey) give you energy

3. PROTEINS (e.g. meat, eggs, nuts, beans) build your muscles and help your body grow and repair

4. FIBRE (e.g. vegetables, fruit, wholegrains) keeps your gut healthy and strong

Food also needs to include
13 special CHEMICALS called VITAMINS.
The body cannot make most of these
chemicals itself, and they are very
important for GOOD HEALTH.

~

In one lifetime
the average human
eats 50 tonnes
of food.

WATER

is an essential
part of our diet.
About two-thirds
of the water in our
body comes from
drinking. Most of
the other third
comes from water
in our foods.

We swallow air as we eat, and this
mostly escapes back up the throat
as a **BURP**. The sound of a burp
comes from the throat wobbling
as the air escapes.

There are about 2 kg of
BACTERIA living in an adult's
digestive system – that's
heavier than their brain!
The bacteria help digest
our food and keep us healthy.

~

Bacteria cells are much
smaller than human cells.
There are 10 bacteria living on
or inside your body for every
one of your own cells.

BACTERIA
in the intestines turn
food waste into **SMELLY
GASES**, which parp
out as **FARTS**. It is
normal to do about
20 farts a day.

Excuse
me!

71

The average person
produces 7 tonnes of
poo in their lifetime.

~

Poo gets its brown colour from an
unwanted chemical that is removed from
the blood and mixed into the poo in the
large intestine. Without this chemical,
poo would look much paler.

IT CAN TAKE ANYWHERE FROM 10 HOURS TO THREE DAYS FOR FOOD TO PASS THROUGH THE HUMAN GUT.

TODAY WE MOSTLY THINK OF PEE AND POO AS DIRTY, UNPLEASANT WASTE, BUT NOT EVERYONE WOULD AGREE ...

FOUR SURPRISING USES FOR PEE AND POO:

The ancient Romans used pee as a tooth-whitening mouthwash.

In the 1100s, ancient Chinese soldiers loaded catapults with burning poo.

For hundreds of years, people used pee to wash their clothes.

In the 1600s, a chemist called Robert Boyle used powdered poo to treat eye disease.

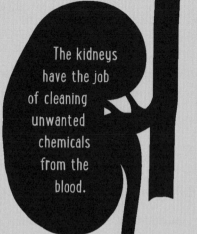

The kidneys have the job of cleaning unwanted chemicals from the blood.

Every day, the kidneys filter the blood 38 times and create a liquid waste, urine – or pee!

Your pee is stored in a stretchy bag called the bladder. When it gets half full you'll begin to feel like it's time to go to the toilet.

~ EVERY YEAR ~
A PERSON PEES OUT
500 LITRES OF URINE.

THAT IS ENOUGH
TO COMPLETELY
FILL

TWO
BATHTUBS.

Transport
Systems

THE BLOOD

is the body's main transport system.

~

It carries food and oxygen around the body.

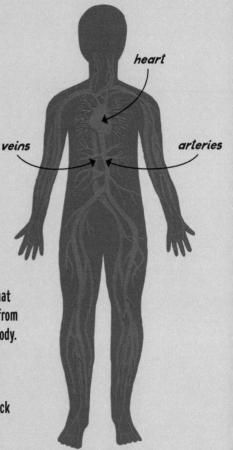

heart

veins

arteries

ARTERIES
are the blood vessels that carry oxygen-rich blood from your heart around your body.

VEINS
are the blood vessels that carry the blood back to the heart.

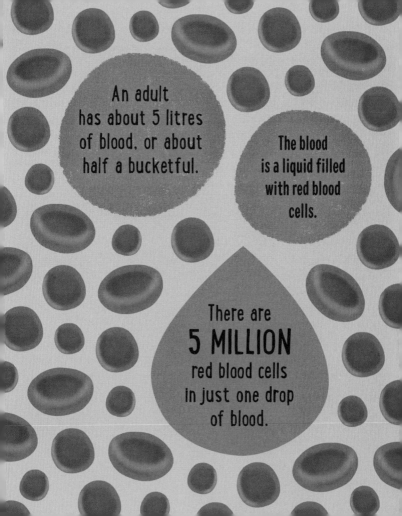

An adult has about 5 litres of blood, or about half a bucketful.

The blood is a liquid filled with red blood cells.

There are **5 MILLION** red blood cells in just one drop of blood.

BLOOD IS RED

because of the red blood cells it contains. The cells are red because they contain a red chemical, which also contains iron, that allows them to pick up oxygen.

Red blood cells carry oxygen
around the body.

~

The blood holds
about 1 LITRE of
OXYGEN at a time –
enough to fill a
party balloon.

~

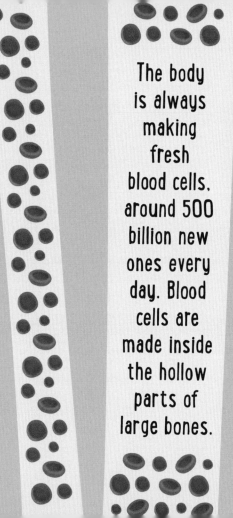

The body
is always
making
fresh
blood cells,
around 500
billion new
ones every
day. Blood
cells are
made inside
the hollow
parts of
large bones.

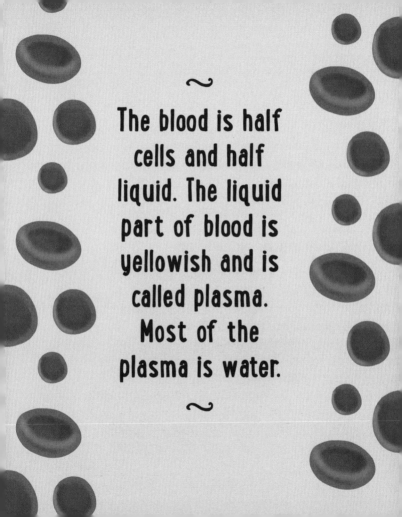

The blood is half cells and half liquid. The liquid part of blood is yellowish and is called plasma. Most of the plasma is water.

The HEART is a hollow PUMP of thick muscles that squeezes on the blood inside, pushing it around the body. The heart has four chambers inside, and the blood moves through each one in a set order.

First it flows to the lungs, where it picks up oxygen, and then loops back to the heart.

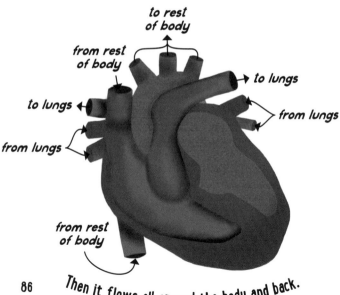

to rest of body

from rest of body

to lungs

to lungs

from lungs

from lungs

from rest of body

Then it flows all around the body and back.

The human heart BEATS about 2.5 to 3 billion times in a lifetime.

The length of all the blood vessels in the body is 96,000 km, more than enough to go around the world twice.

Breathing allows air to flow in and out.

A normal breathing rate is about 15 breaths every minute. When you are running, the rate goes up to about 50 breaths a minute.

BREATHING FILLS THE LUNGS WITH AIR.

The lungs are spongy bags filled with many branching air tubes. If all the lungs' tubes were joined together, they would stretch 2,400 km, which is the length of India!

Each of the air tubes
in the lungs ends in a
little round sac called
an **ALVEOLUS**.

~

Each alveolus is tiny
– just 0.5 mm wide.

The lungs take oxygen from the air and pass it into the blood. This happens in the alveolus. There are 480 million of them inside human lungs.

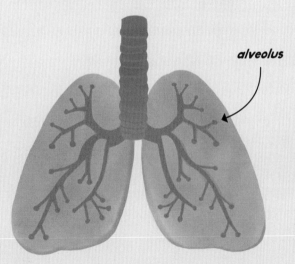

alveolus

The air we breathe in is
ONE-FIFTH OXYGEN GAS
(almost all the rest is NITROGEN
GAS). The air we breathe out is
only about ONE-SIXTH OXYGEN
because the lungs have replaced
some of it with a waste gas
called CARBON DIOXIDE.

The oxygen our lungs take from the air is used to make energy.

We breathe in through our mouth and nose, and the air goes down the windpipe and into the lungs.

We also use our mouth for eating. To make sure food doesn't go down the windpipe and into the lungs, a flap called the epiglottis closes the windpipe when we swallow.

We do not need to think about breathing. It happens automatically as a big muscle under the lungs called the **DIAPHRAGM** moves up and down to pump air in and out of the body.

A yawn is a sudden big in-breath that happens without much warning. Yawning becomes more common as we get tired, but no one really knows why we do it.

Yawning is contagious, which means that when we see someone else yawn it makes us feel like yawning too – and it is hard to stop ourselves.

95

～ A HICCUP ～

happens when your diaphragm and rib muscles suddenly contract (pull), causing you to breathe in very suddenly, which makes a noise, while your epiglottis shuts.

During a **SNEEZE** or COUGH, air rushes out of the nose at 16 km an hour.

1.
Dust

2.
Pollen

3.
Pepper or
spicy food

~

FIVE THINGS
that can make
you sneeze (apart
from illness):

4.
Bright
light

5.
Plucking your
eyebrows

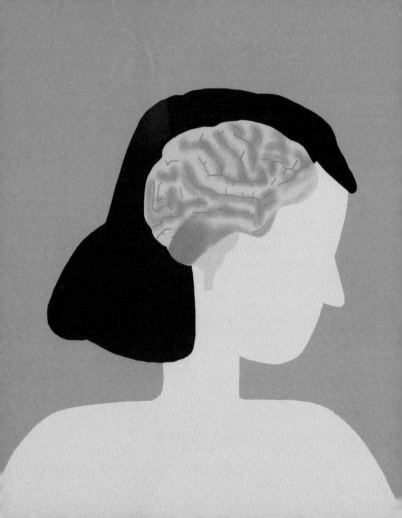

The
Brain and
Senses

THE BRAIN is the
control centre of the body.
It organises all the other organs. It is
made mostly of water and fat.

An adult's
brain weighs
about 1.3 kg.

A fully grown brain has **83 BILLION** nerve cells in it, and each one is connected to hundreds of its neighbours.

There are **100 TRILLION** connections in the human brain, more than the number of stars in the galaxy!

THE BRAIN sends and
receives signals as ELECTRIC PULSES
travelling along wire-like cells called nerves.
The signals can travel along the nerve at
about 80 m a second, about as fast
as a Formula One race car.

A NEWBORN BABY'S BRAIN AND NERVES
ARE NOT FULLY CONNECTED UP. THE NERVES
LINK TOGETHER AS THE BABY LEARNS TO
STAND UP AND WALK AROUND.

~

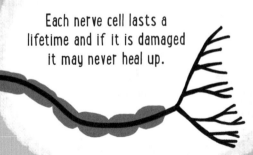

It takes more than
20 years for the body's
nerves to grow fully.

Each nerve cell lasts a
lifetime and if it is damaged
it may never heal up.

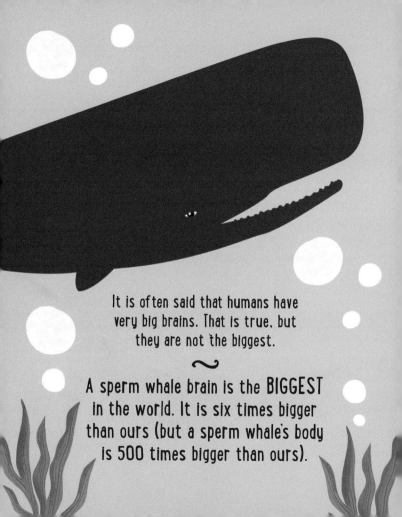

It is often said that humans have very big brains. That is true, but they are not the biggest.

A sperm whale brain is the BIGGEST in the world. It is six times bigger than ours (but a sperm whale's body is 500 times bigger than ours).

The human brain makes up one-fortieth of our body weight. An ant's brain is much bigger for its size. It makes up one-seventh of its body weight.

YOU THINK AROUND **20,000** THOUGHTS A DAY.

Learning can actually change the shape of your brain!

Kids who learn two languages before the age of five use a larger area of their brains to process words than people who speak just one language.

TAXI DRIVERS, who memorise hundreds of routes, often build up the part of the brain that handles their awareness of place and direction.

Running down your backbone is a thick bundle of nerves called the spinal cord. It connects the brain to the body.

~

A reflex is a special movement that happens automatically. Most reflexes are controlled by the spinal cord, not the brain.

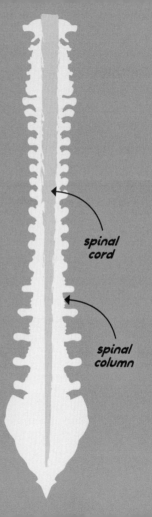

spinal cord

spinal column

108

SIX REFLEX ACTIONS:

~

- Blinking
- Shivering
- Moving away from something hot or sharp
- Sneezing
- Putting your hands out as you fall over

zzzZZZ Z

Your brain stays very
active while you sleep.

No one really knows what it is doing.
Your heartbeat and breathing slow right
down and your muscles relax.
but your brain
stays busy.

The **LOUDEST** snoring ever recorded was 93 decibels, which is about as loud as an electric lawn mower!

zᶻᶻZ

Scientists still do not know why humans and other animals have to go to sleep. Some people think their brain is tidying up after the day's activities.

The human
eye is an EGG SHAPE
about 2.5 cm wide.

~

It is already two-thirds
grown when a baby is born
and reaches its full size
at the age of 13.

~

It can detect 10 million
different shades
of colour.

Brown eyes get their colour

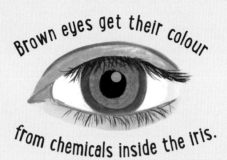

from chemicals inside the iris.

Blue, grey and green eyes do not

have these coloured chemicals.

Instead they get their colours
from the way light shines
through the iris.

THE EYE PICKS UP LIGHT USING SPECIAL LIGHT-DETECTING CELLS INSIDE IT.

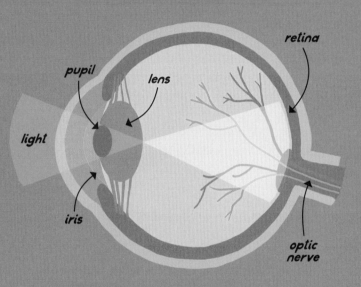

Light enters the eye through a hole called the pupil, and is beamed onto light-detecting cells at the back of the eye (the retina).

Signals pass from the
light-detecting cells along
a big nerve – called the
optic nerve – to the brain.

~

The brain combines the
signals to create a colour
picture of the world.

Sound is a vibration running through the air. A flap of skin called the EARDRUM inside the ear WOBBLES in time with the sound vibration as the air hits it.

The wobble of the eardrum makes three TINY BONES – the smallest in the body – tap out sound onto a snail-shaped structure filled with liquid. The vibrations in the liquid are sent by nerves to the brain.

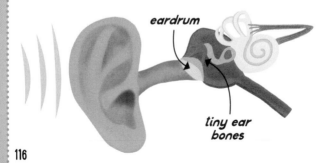

eardrum

tiny ear bones

Having two ears means you can work out which direction a sound is coming from.

The structures inside the ear are not just used for hearing.

The way the liquid flows back and forth inside is used by the brain to detect which way the body is moving so it can keep balanced.

~

When liquid in the ear is swirling around too much, the brain gets CONFUSED and we feel DIZZY!

119

THE NOSE picks up
smelly chemicals using 1,000
types of cell deep inside it.

Together these cells can
pick up more than 100,000
different kinds of smells.

A DOG'S
sense of smell
is around 10,000
TIMES better
than ours.

THE TONGUE'S TASTE BUDS CAN PICK UP FIVE TASTES:

sweet, sour, bitter, salty and another savoury taste called umami.

~

The taste of chilli is not a taste at all. Instead the spice makes the mouth feel hot!

Your skin has thousands of **TOUCH DETECTORS** that allow you to touch and feel the world. There are 3,000 in each fingertip alone.

~

People feel the cold more in autumn than in spring – even if the temperature is the same. This is because their skin has become used to being warm during summer.

THERE ARE SIX TYPES OF TOUCH DETECTORS, WHICH PICK UP:

1. Light touch
2. Hard press
3. Squeezing
4. Stretching
5. Cold
6. Heat

Attack
and
Defence

~ **SKIN** ~

is the first line
of defence
protecting you
against damage
and disease, and
it is your body's
largest organ.

The outer layer
of skin is completely
dead. It is made
from layers of dead
cells filled with a
waterproof waxy
chemical.

The dead skin cells
are constantly falling
off and being replaced.
Every minute, 2 million
skin cells fall off you.

~

Most of the dust in
your home is flakes of
dead skin. The whole
surface of the skin is
renewed every month.

There are about 100,000 hairs growing on the head and there are another 5 million much smaller ones on the rest of the body.

HAIR COLOUR COMES FROM TWO CHEMICALS INSIDE IT. ONE IS BLACK, THE OTHER IS RED.

~

Black hair: black colour

Brown hair: black colour
+ red colour

Blonde hair: Small amounts
of both colours

Red hair: red colour

White hair: no colour
chemicals at all

A strand of hair is dead, so you do not feel anything when it is cut. It is made from many layers of KERATIN, the same waxy material that makes the skin waterproof. Keratin is also used to make FINGERNAILS and TOENAILS, FEATHERS, HORNS, HOOVES, SCALES and BEAKS.

keratin horn

Hair grows at about 1.5 cm a month. It stops growing after about 6 years when it is around 1 m long – and then most likely falls out.

FINGERNAILS
grow about 3 mm a month, which is about twice as fast as toenails.

The **EYELASHES** work as curtains that protect the eye by stopping dust from getting into it. Blinking wipes away any specks that get through. People blink 6 million times a year!

～ TEARS ～

come from glands above the eye and drain into the corner of the eye. They are used to wash the surface of the eye clean – and also come out when we cry!

One-third of people
have tiny mites living
on their eyelashes. These
eyelash mites are a third
of a millimetre long and
eat the oils used to keep
the hairs flexible.

The only body parts with no hair
at all are the **palms of the hands**,
soles of the feet and the lips.

~

The skin on the palms has tiny **bumps**
and **ridges** that form flexible, fleshy
pads. These pads mould around objects
to make it easier to hold on to them.

~

The shape of the ridges on the skin
on the fingertips make a unique
fingerprint. No one else
has the same fingerprints as you,
not even if you have an
identical twin.

135

Small holes in the
skin give out a salty
liquid called **sweat**,
which helps keep
the body cool.

~

EVERY DAY THE BODY
PRODUCES ABOUT A
LITRE OF SWEAT.

MUCUS,
also known as snot,
is a sticky liquid that coats
the soft lining of the nose
and throat, keeping it
clean and moist.
Most of it trickles down
into the stomach.

The proper name for
EARWAX
is cerumen. It collects
dirt and dust, keeping
the ear clean.

If the skin gets cut or grazed, the body's defence system springs into action. A scab starts to form. Its job is to seal up cuts in the skin.

~

Blood fills the cut and then special blood cells called platelets stick together, making a crust called a clot, which fills in the gap. The scab will stop germs getting into the body while the skin heals back.

Scabs itch because the skin around them gets tight and dry as the cut heals up. **DON'T PICK!**

As well as the red blood cells, the blood contains cells known as

WHITE BLOOD CELLS - although they are really many different colours. White blood cells defend the body from attack by viruses and bacteria.

bacteria

white blood cell

Many infectious diseases, such as colds, flu, chickenpox and COVID are caused by viruses. These tiny invaders are about 50 thousandths of a millimetre across, many times smaller than bacteria. You could fit 20,000 of them across the width of a human hair.

coronavirus

An allergy is when the body's white blood cells fight against something harmless.

For example, hay fever happens when they attack pollen in the air that has got into the body.

142

A **vaccine** is a medicine that teaches the **white blood cells** how to defend the body against a particular **disease** before it can do **damage** or even **kill you**. Vaccines prevent at least 2.5 million people from dying from serious diseases every year.

∿

Most vaccines are given as an **injection**, but some are squirted up the **nose**, and others can be eaten as **sweets!**

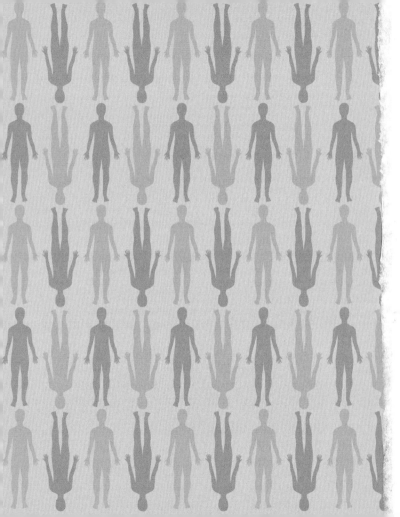